AF365421

Special thanks to
Griet and **Ann** for
their friendship and
support while making
this book and for the
transformational
and powerful inner healing
I have experienced at
the labyrinth in
lasendacostarica.com

Text copyright © 2019
Carmen Martínez Jover
www.carmenmartinezjover.com
Illustrations copyright © August 2020
Carmen Martínez Jover

Soul's Time to be Born,
an adoption story for girls
ISBN -978-607-29-2250-1

Story & Illustrations:
Carmen Martínez Jover
Layout & text layout:
Víctor Nieto
flippon@gmail.com

Nicole
I dedicate this story to you.

Thank you for choosing to be in my
world and walking alongside me through the
challenges that life presents us.
I am so proud of you and grateful to have
you in my life. Travelling and creating this
book together with you, Nicole, has been
the most blissful experience ever!

I love you so much!
Mum

Soul's
Time
to
be
Born
Written and Illustrated by Carmen Martinez Jover

Matilda was a beautiful soul and lived very happily in the spirit realm.

Connected to source, feeling peaceful, grateful and surrounded by unconditional love.

here she gathered with her soul group.
Some had been with her before and others
were ready to accompany her in the future.
Some had even agreed to help through
the ups and downs of life.

Matilda's time had come to be born, so she went to visit the Elders and together they helped plan her new life.
The time was perfect, and the Elders gave her some important advice before she left.

The Elders said…

"Matilda, when you
are born remember to:
be happy, love nature,
be grateful, meditate,
live the present moment,
love and be loved, smile,
be spiritual, laugh,
dream, be fearless,
have fun, forgive,
connect, listen,
care for others,
be yourself,
be kind."

She could have been born in many
Matilda was then taken to see several life options.

different countries, had different religions and could have even been a boy or girl.

In those options,
Matilda saw
Didi and Canik
for the first time.

She saw flashes of
what her life would be
with them as her parents,
one full of adventure
and challenges, days of
laughter and also
some tears, but always
filled with lots of love.

The life she chose
started with quite
a challenge.

Matilda was explained how she couldn't
be born in a conventional way, so she'd
need to find another lady's tummy in
which to be born. Once born, she'd
be able to make her way to her chosen
parents with the help of adoption.

So, **Matilda** accepted the challenge.

Matilda started her journey from spirit realm…

To womb...
To Didi & Canik

Matilda enjoyed being with her parents.

Souls
Time to be
Born

Matilda grew… and grew… and grew… and grew…
and lived happily facing the ups and downs of life, surrounded by her parents and friends.

Remember
what the Elder's said.

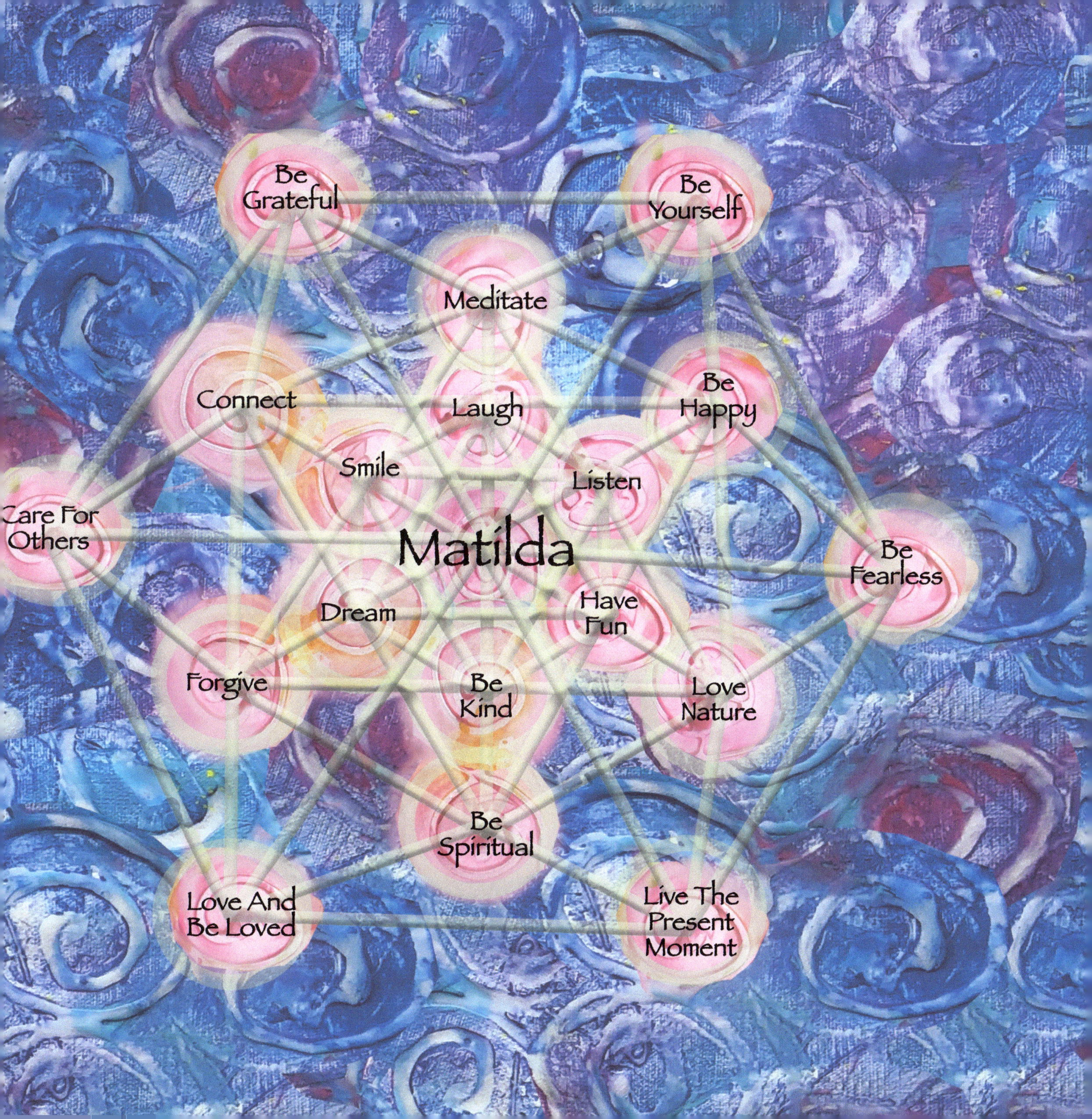

Be
Grateful
Be
Yourself
Meditate
Connect
Laugh
Be
Happy
Smile
Listen
Care For
Others
Matilda
Be
Fearless
Dream
Have
Fun
Forgive
Be
Kind
Love
Nature
Be
Spiritual
Love And
Be Loved
Live The
Present
Moment

Matilda's
tips to
happiness

1 Sit down and make yourself comfortable.
2 Close your eyes and take 3 deep breaths.
3 Listen to your heartbeat. Relax.
4 Smile. Feel it in your heart.
5 Remember and visualise 10 things you are grateful for.

Mum
Fertility Coach
Int'l Lecturer
Author
Therapist
Artist
The roots of her worst nightmare became her biggest blessing!
Hormones
Too many failed IVFs
Injections
Depression
This is Carmen's story…

Personalise Your Own Book
books.carmenmartinezjover.com
Two Dads
I Want To Have a Child
Egg Donation
Recipes of How Babies are Made
Adoption
Single Mum by Choice
*Available in: English, Español, Français, Italiano, русский, Português, Polsku, & Deutsch